Celestial Awakening: Ascension and the Art of Summoning UFOs

Jessie Contreras

Published by Summon UFOs, 2024.

CELESTIAL AWAKENING: ASCENSION AND THE ART OF SUMMONING UFOS

First edition. September 12, 2024.

Copyright © 2024 Jessie Contreras.

ISBN: 979-8227635907

Written by Jessie Contreras.

"To all aspiring UFO summoners, may your hearts be open and your spirits fearless as you embark on this extraordinary journey. This book is dedicated to your quest for connection with the cosmos, where the mysteries of the universe await. Trust in your intuition, embrace the unknown, and remember that each step taken in pursuit of the extraordinary brings you closer to the stars. May your journeys be filled with wonder and enlightenment."

1. The Call of the Unknown

1.1 My First Encounter with the Unknown

The night sky was a deep canvas of indigo, speckled with stars that seemed to pulse with ancient energy. On that fateful evening, while taking a quiet stroll, I felt an undeniable pull—something was different. Suddenly, there it was: a shimmering light, darting effortlessly across the horizon. My heart raced as I instinctively knew this was no ordinary aircraft. It glowed with a brilliance that was both mesmerizing and surreal, leaving me utterly breathless. I stood frozen in awe, captivated not only by the sight itself but by the profound sense of wonder that enveloped me. This experience transcended any earthly explanation. It was an encounter with the unknown, a moment of pure connection to something larger than myself. The UFO seemed to dance, shifting colors and patterns as if communicating with me directly. I was left questioning everything I thought I understood about reality.

This moment sparked a flame within me, igniting a journey of spiritual exploration that I yearned to pursue. I began diving into books about extraterrestrial life, conspiracy theories, and ancient civilizations that spoke of cosmic visitors. Each new piece of information opened doors to questions I had never thought to ask. What if we are not alone? What if the universe is teeming with life just beyond our perception? My heart longed for more than the mundane existence I had lived thus far. I started meditating, seeking connections beyond the physical realm, and even tried various methods to summon these beings. This desire to explore the unknown transformed my life, leading me down paths I could never have envisioned before that night. With each new discovery, I felt more connected to the universe and the mysteries it holds.

When seeking your own encounters or understanding of the unknown, it's important to approach with an open heart and mind. Engage in practices that enhance your intuition, such as journaling your dreams or spending time in nature. Cultivating a sense of wonder and reverence for the universe can create the right conditions for these extraordinary experiences. Remember, the journey itself can be as enlightening as the destination.

1.2 Understanding the Attraction to UFOs

There is a powerful, universal pull that many of us feel towards the mysteries of the sky. Each star, twinkling in the vastness, seems to whisper secrets just out of reach. I remember my first encounter with the night sky, lying on a blanket in my backyard, gazing upward. The endless tapestry of stars ignited a flame of curiosity within me. It's as if we are all connected by an invisible thread, woven through the cosmos, compelling us to question what lies beyond our Earthly realm. The phenomenon of UFOs captures our imagination not merely as visitors from another planet but as symbols of the unknown and perhaps even unexplored aspects of ourselves. This shared intrigue transcends cultural and geographical barriers, uniting us in our quest for understanding. It speaks to a primal human urge to seek out what cannot be easily explained and to connect with something greater than ourselves.

The curiosity about life beyond Earth often intertwines with our spiritual growth. As we ponder the existence of other beings, we are also led to explore our own inner dimensions. I've found that contemplating the possibility of extraterrestrial life can trigger profound reflections on our own purpose and existence. Each thought about a potential cosmic connection stirs a deeper inquiry into who we truly are and why we are here. This isn't just about looking to the stars; it's about looking within and realizing that our spirit yearns for something extraordinary. It encourages us to expand our consciousness and embrace concepts that may feel foreign yet enticing. Engaging with these thoughts can enhance our spiritual journey, inviting us to raise our vibrations and be more open to the enchanted realities around us.

In contemplating UFOs, we awaken a desire to connect with higher dimensions of existence. To foster this connection, it can be useful to spend quiet moments outside, allowing the beauty of the night sky to inspire you. Simple practices like stargazing, meditating under the stars, or even participating in group meditations focused on these themes can help align your energy with the cosmos. As you embark on this journey, trust that your attraction to UFOs can lead you towards self-discovery and spiritual ascension.

1.3 Signs from the Universe: Are You Being Called?

Throughout my journey, I have often found myself experiencing moments that felt way too synchronistic to be mere coincidence. These instances have nudged me to question reality and the forces that might be guiding my path. Have you ever noticed a recurring number, a specific animal crossing your path, or even found that a song plays at just the right moment when you need inspiration? Such synchronicities may signal a calling, a divine tap on the shoulder inviting you to explore deeper realms of existence. For me, these signs led to a realization: every synchronicity is an invitation to engage with the universe and understand what is truly meant for us. I've learned to pay attention to these signs, taking time to reflect on their meanings and the feelings they evoke within me. It's as if the universe is whispering, "Look here, there is something important for you to see." Recognizing these moments can open the door to a richer, more fulfilling life.

To determine if you are meant to pursue UFO summoning, I encourage you to take a step back and reflect on your own experiences. Ask yourself how you feel in the presence of these signs and synchronicities. Are they making your heart race with excitement and hope, or do they cause uncertainty and fear? I recall a particularly powerful instance when I felt an inexplicable urge to go stargazing one clear night. Under the vast, starry sky, I felt a deep connection with the cosmos and an overwhelming desire to reach out. It was in that moment of reflection that I understood this pull wasn't just curiosity—it was a calling. Write down your thoughts, meditate on your feelings, and allow the reflections to guide you. The process doesn't require perfection; rather, it's about understanding where you stand with your multifaceted experiences. Trusting in your intuition can lead the way and help you identify whether your journey includes summoning UFOs.

One practical tip is to start a journal dedicated to your experiences with signs and synchronicities in your life. Documenting these moments can provide clarity and help you notice patterns over time. As you build this record, you might even uncover a deeper connection to your own journey and the cosmic events swirling around you. By engaging with this practice, you make a conscious effort to invite the universe's messages into your awareness, expanding your insight into what it may be trying to communicate.

2. Preparing Your Mind and Spirit

2.1 Meditation Techniques for High Vibration

Meditation practices are powerful tools in elevating our vibrational frequency, allowing us to connect more deeply with ourselves and the universe. One of the techniques that really transformed my journey is mindfulness meditation. This practice involves focusing on the present moment and observing thoughts without judgment. As I began to cultivate this awareness, I noticed how my vibration naturally started to rise. The key is to create a space where you can tune into your inner self, allowing the distractions of daily life to fade into the background. Another effective technique is guided visualization, where I immerse myself in vivid imagery of light and energy. Visualizing myself surrounded by radiant light not only enhances my mood but also aligns my energy with higher realms, inviting an uplifting experience. Breathwork is yet another invaluable addition to my practice. Concentrating on my breath, inhaling deeply and exhaling slowly, helps center my energy and clear stagnant vibrations, making way for higher frequencies to seep in.

Through my own experiences with meditation, I've discovered that it deepens my connection to higher realms in unexpected ways. During these quiet moments, insights and ideas flood into my consciousness that feel like they're coming from beyond me. Once, while in a deep meditative state, I felt a profound sense of unity with the universe, as if I were floating among the stars. It was in this space that I sensed the presence of other beings, perhaps extraterrestrial, guiding me and urging me to explore further. Each session feels like a cosmic invitation, opening doors to inter-dimensional connections that thrill me to my core. These moments are often accompanied by flashes of inspiration regarding my own spiritual journey and my desire to summon UFOs. The deeper I delve into meditation, the clearer my intentions become, and the more attuned I feel to these extraordinary experiences. It's as if the veil has been lifted just enough for me to glimpse what lies beyond.

Every time I meditate, it's an opportunity to reach an elevated state of consciousness. I encourage you to try incorporating these techniques into your routine. Set up a dedicated space, free from interruptions, and fully commit to the experience. Let your mind wander, trust the process, and embrace whatever arises, be it insight, energy shifts, or even unexpected contact. Remember, every journey is unique, and your vibration will rise naturally as you explore the depths of your meditative practice. When you maintain an open heart and mind, the universe responds in kind—providing connections, interactions, and the extraordinary visions that your spirit is longing for.

2.2 Setting Intentions: The Power of Your Mind

Clear intentions are crucial in the UFO summoning process because they act as a guiding compass for our thoughts and actions. When I began my journey, I realized that if I didn't have a specific intention, my energy was scattered and unfocused. Setting a clear intention helps to align my inner energy with my outer manifestations. Each time I focused my mind on a particular outcome, I found that my experiences became more meaningful. It was as if the universe was responding to my inner dialogue, reflecting my desires back to me. This clarity pulls in the energies that vibrate at the same frequency as my intention, creating a powerful synergy that enhances the likelihood of encounter. As I reflected on my experiences, it became clear that vague wishes yielded vague results, while laser-focused intentions produced remarkable outcomes. The strength of our thoughts in this process is profound; they shape our reality more than we often realize.

I experimented with several intention-setting techniques that fueled my personal success in summoning UFOs. One technique that worked exceptionally well for me was visualization. I would sit in a serene environment, close my eyes, and visualize myself in the presence of a UFO. I imagined every detail—the colors, the sounds, the feeling of awe and wonder. This deep mental engagement helped me establish a connection with the phenomenon I wanted to attract. Another technique involved scripting my experiences as if they had already happened. I would write down a detailed account of a successful meeting with a UFO, describing what I saw, how it felt, and what messages were shared. By documenting my desired experiences, I created a mental placeholder that made them feel more real and attainable. Additionally, I employed meditation to enter a calm, receptive state that allowed me to send out my intentions more clearly. Each practice reinforced my commitment and belief, enhancing my capacity to connect with the unknown.

As you explore intention-setting, consider embracing a ritual that resonates with you personally. Whether it's lighting a candle while stating your intention aloud or creating a vision board filled with images of what you seek, the key is to infuse these practices with genuine emotion. Feel what it would be like to achieve your desires, and use that energy as fuel for your intentions. This way, your mind and heart work in tandem, amplifying the power of your craft.

2.3 Cleansing Your Space: Creating a Sanctuary

Cleansing your physical and spiritual space is vital for inviting higher energies and creating a harmonious environment. I often start by decluttering my surroundings. It's amazing how much energy stagnant items can hold. Aside from the physical mess, lingering emotions or memories tied to objects can also weigh us down. By simplifying my space, I create a clean slate, allowing new energy to flow freely. Next, I turn to arrangement—ensuring that the furniture and decor support positive energy flow. I find that facing my bed toward the door, for example, creates a sense of safety and openness, enhancing my spiritual experience. Fresh air also plays a key role in cleansing; I like to open the windows wide to let the breeze sweep through, symbolically washing away any dense energy.

Transitioning to spiritual cleansing, I have a few rituals that truly work for me. Burning sage or sweetgrass is one of my favorites. The smoke carries away negativity and invites protection while filling the space with sacredness. I follow up with salt water, a powerful natural cleanser. A simple ritual involves sprinkling salt water around the room and visualizing it absorbing any unwanted energy. For those nights when I'm setting the stage for UFO summoning, I create an inviting atmosphere. I often utilize crystals, arranging them in a circle to amplify energy. The gemstones serve as conduits, enhancing my intentions and helping me connect with higher realms. Soft lighting with candles or colored LED lights adds to the mood, creating a welcoming space for both earthly beings and potential visitors from above.

Ultimately, the process of cleansing is not static; it evolves with my needs and intentions. Therefore, regularly revisiting my space and rituals keeps my environment aligned with my spiritual journey. Yesterday, while summoning, it hit me how critical the atmosphere felt. The combination of lavender incense and a cool breeze seemed to elevate the whole experience, as the cosmos responded in kind. For anyone interested in working with the energies of the universe, creating and cleansing a sanctuary is essential. Remember, the intention you set will resonate strongly; so, approach each ritual with mindfulness and clarity. A practical tip: consider incorporating sound, like chimes or soothing music, to clear stale energy and uplift your space.

3. The Art of Summoning

3.1 Energy Alignment: Tuning into the Right Frequency

Energy alignment is a profound concept that often feels elusive yet is critical when it comes to summoning. It's like tuning an old radio; if you don't find the exact frequency, all you'll hear is static. The essence of energy alignment lies in harmonizing our own vibrations with the frequencies that resonate with the universe, particularly those of our cosmic allies. It's about becoming aware of our inner energies and adjusting them to create a powerful connection. When I learned to align my energy, I noticed that it not only opened doors to deeper experiences but also heightened my ability to connect with others on a spiritual level. This alignment makes us more receptive to signs and signals from beyond, facilitating a seamless communication path that invites otherworldly beings into our sphere.

My journey to discovering my personal frequencies began unexpectedly. There were countless nights spent in silence, observing the stars and listening to the whispers of the universe. I experimented with meditation techniques, sound healing, and nature walks, each offering unique insights into my own energy patterns. Some nights, I would stand outside under the vastness of the sky, seeking connections, and suddenly, I would feel a subtle vibration in my chest or a tingling sensation in my fingertips. I began to understand that my state of mind and emotional resonance played a vital role in this cosmic dance. The more I tuned into these sensations, the clearer my connection became. It felt like a conversation without words, a dance of energies where understanding flowed effortlessly. Over time, my practice of energy alignment transformed, becoming a ritual I cherished and deeply respected.

Creating space for these frequencies is essential. I learned that grounding myself before each session was crucial to receive clearer messages from the cosmos. Simple practices like deep breathing, walking barefoot on the earth, or visualizing a bright light surrounding me helped me achieve a state of openness. What I found particularly fascinating was how my mood directly influenced my capacity to connect. When I aligned my energy with positivity and gratitude, the results were astounding. I would often journal my experiences, noting how variations in my emotional state affected my cosmic interactions. Trusting in these experiences taught me that we all have unique frequencies waiting to be discovered. To facilitate your own summoning experiences, consider developing a routine that enhances your energy alignment. Experiment patiently with meditation, mindfulness, and self-reflection, as these practices can reveal the frequencies that resonate deeply within you. Embrace the journey, and you may find the stars responding in ways you never thought possible.

3.2 Creating a Summoning Ritual

Crafting your own summoning ritual can be a transformative experience, allowing you to connect with energies beyond our physical realm. The first step in creating a ritual is to determine your intention. Think about what you wish to summon. It could be knowledge, energy, or perhaps direct contact with a UFO. Once you have a clear purpose, the next step is to gather your materials. Elements like candles, crystals, and herbs can enhance the energy you're trying to harness. Choose items that resonate with your intention; for instance, if you're aiming to connect with extraterrestrial beings, blue or silver candles might symbolize communication. You'll also want a quiet space where you can focus without interruptions, perhaps outside under the stars where you'll be closer to the celestial bodies.

Personalization is key to the effectiveness of any ritual. No two practitioners are the same, and your unique experiences and beliefs shape the energy you create. Think about what symbols or rituals have personal significance for you. This could involve incorporating music that elevates your spirit, wearing specific clothing that makes you feel empowered, or using imagery that inspires your intention. When you infuse your ritual with personal meaning, it resonates deeper, making it a reflection of your authentic self. The more you engage emotionally with your setup, the more powerful the experience tends to be. It's also beneficial to keep a journal of your rituals, as tracking your experiences can illuminate patterns and enhance your understanding of the process.

When you finally perform your ritual, approach it with the mindset that you are opening a channel to the universe. Speak your intentions clearly and confidently, visualizing the energy flowing towards your goal. After you've concluded your ritual, take time to reflect and be open to the signs and sensations that follow. They may not always be immediate, but remaining receptive to unexpected experiences can lead to profound encounters. As a practical tip, consider regularly revisiting and rewriting your ritual, adapting it as you learn and evolve on your journey of ascension and connection with the cosmos.

3.3 Tools for Enhanced Connection: Crystals and More

Crystals have a unique ability to amplify energies and intentions, and they play a significant role in enhancing my UFO summoning experiences. Each crystal vibrates at its own frequency, creating a connection to specific energies that can aid in communication with otherworldly beings. For me, using crystals such as clear quartz, amethyst, and labradorite has been transformative. Clear quartz is known for its ability to amplify intentions, making it an excellent choice for enhancing psychic abilities. Amethyst adds a layer of spiritual protection, while labradorite opens the gateway to intuition and other dimensions. I often lay these crystals out in a specific pattern when I prepare for summoning, allowing them to create a resonant field that feels conducive to the experience I am seeking.

Choosing the right crystal or object for your personal practice is key to deepening your connection. First, tune into your own intuition; you might find that certain stones call to you more than others. When you select a crystal, hold it in your hand and take a moment to observe how it feels. Is there a warmth or tingling sensation? That can be a sign that there's a resonance between you and the crystal. Once selected, cleansing your crystals is essential. I usually smudge them with sage or place them under running water to clear any previous energies. After cleansing, sit quietly with your crystal and meditate on your intention. Whether it's connecting with extraterrestrial energies or expanding your consciousness, focus your thoughts as you hold your stone. Consider incorporating other objects that carry significance for you, such as feathers or small talismans, as they can also enhance your energetic field.

Always keep in mind that the intention you set is more powerful than the tools you use. Crystals and other objects serve as conduits for energy, but your focus and openness are what truly make the connection. When summoning UFOs, create a sacred space where you feel comfortable and safe. This could be indoors or outdoors, wherever you feel drawn to. Arrange your crystals and objects in a way that feels harmonious to you. Pay attention to your thoughts and emotions, as they can influence the experience. To elevate your practice, consider journaling your experiences. Document what you feel, see, and intuit after each session. Over time, you may notice patterns, messages, or even signs from your extraterrestrial visitors. Trust in your journey and remember that every step taken with intention brings you closer to the cosmic connection you seek.

4. Understanding the UFO Phenomenon

4.1 Types of UFOs and Their Characteristics

Throughout my journey into the realms of the unknown, I've encountered various types of UFOs, each marked by distinct characteristics that often resonate with deeper spiritual meanings. Some may be craft-like, metallic and sleek, while others exhibit softer, glowing forms that seem almost ethereal. Each type can signify different aspects of our spiritual journey and consciousness. For instance, disk-shaped UFOs often evoke thoughts of advanced technology and higher knowledge, suggesting an invitation to explore the limits of our understanding and to reach for enlightenment. In contrast, orbs of light evoke a sense of peace and interconnectedness, symbolizing the essence of love and unity that transcends our three-dimensional existence. The varied shapes and colors of UFOs can reflect the multifaceted nature of our own souls, urging us to consider what these manifestations may reveal about our own journeys toward ascension.

During one summer night, I stood outside, gazing up at the stars when I noticed a flickering light moving eerily across the sky. At first, I thought it might be an airplane, but as it changed direction abruptly and ascended vertically, I felt a mixture of fear and fascination. This UFO had characteristics that I would later learn to recognize as typical of interdimensional craft. In that moment, it felt as if I was being drawn into a cosmic dance, one that communicated a deeper message about the synchronicity of the Universe. Another more profound encounter unfolded during a meditation retreat when, as I closed my eyes, a vivid vision of a golden, pulsating orb filled my mind. It radiated warmth, sparking feelings of unconditional love and connection. When I emerged from meditation, I was startled to find that many participants had experienced similar visions, and discussions swirled around the idea that these experiences could represent a collective awakening or spiritual summoning. It was in these moments of connection that I truly began to appreciate the role these phenomena play in our spiritual evolution.

These personal stories underscore how each encounter with UFOs invites us to explore the depths of our spiritual understanding and further encourages us to engage with the unknown. The next time you find yourself under the vast night sky, remain open to the possibility of witnessing something extraordinary. Acknowledge that these experiences may not just be random occurrences, but instead powerful messages from the Universe. Engaging in meditative practices before stargazing can enhance your sensitivity to these phenomena. By aligning your energy with the higher vibrations of the Universe, you may tune into the subtle signals that help guide your spiritual journey.

4.2 Historical Accounts and Their Messages

Throughout history, there have been countless encounters with unidentified flying objects that have left an indelible mark on our collective consciousness. Many of these accounts, ranging from ancient texts to modern-day sightings, carry profound spiritual messages. Taking a moment to explore these encounters reveals patterns that often transcend the simple surprise of seeing an unknown craft. For instance, Native American legends speak of star people, ethereal beings who came to Earth to share wisdom and insight. Similarly, the biblical accounts of chariots of fire can be seen as an early testament to divine visitors from the sky, urging humanity to pursue a higher path. When I delve into these stories, I am struck by the recurring theme that these encounters serve as a catalyst for spiritual awakening, inviting us to embrace the unknown and seek deeper truths about our purpose in the universe.

These narratives extend beyond mere fascination; they provide a roadmap for understanding our present and future. Each historical UFO sighting often embodies a call to action, inspiring individuals and communities to reconsider their relationship with the cosmos. In my own journey of ascension, I've noticed how the revelations from these accounts can reshape our practices and beliefs. They encourage openness to the unseen and an understanding that we are part of a greater tapestry. Engaging with these stories allows us to reflect on our spiritual growth and invites us to establish connections with higher frequencies of existence. By embracing the wisdom inherent in these accounts, we can refine our spiritual practices to align with the universal messages that consistently emerge from these encounters.

Understanding historical UFO encounters can significantly enhance our journey of summoning these phenomena. When we incorporate the lessons from the past—lessons of trust, unity, and courage—we pave the way for transformative experiences. Practice makes perfect; consider documenting your own spontaneous thoughts and feelings as you meditate on these narratives. Engage with them through visualization or create rituals that honor the spiritual messages they convey. By actively participating in this process, you can heighten your vibrational state and become more attuned to the frequencies of the cosmos. The historical accounts serve as both a guide and a motivation, prompting us to look up to the skies and connect, just as those who came before us did.

4.3 UFOs and Extraterrestrial Life: A Spiritual Perspective

Examining the connection between UFOs and the existence of extraterrestrial beings leads us into a deeper understanding of our universe. Many people have witnessed unidentified flying objects, and those sightings often ignite a sense of wonder and possibility. This curiosity can prompt us to ponder whether these mysterious vessels are harbingers from other worlds or dimensions. Personally, every time I have looked up at the night sky, I felt a connection to something greater than myself, something that transcends our earthly existence. The idea that we might not be alone invites exploration into our place in the cosmos and challenges our understanding of life itself. Could these beings be here not only to observe us but also to guide us? There is a fascinating perspective that extraterrestrial beings may serve as teachers of cosmic wisdom. Imagine them as cosmic mentors, imparting knowledge about the universe and our spiritual evolution. For me, the thought of receiving enlightening insights from these advanced beings is both thrilling and humbling. They likely possess knowledge that far surpasses our current understanding, encompassing themes of love, unity, and the interconnectedness of all life forms. Engaging with these beings during meditative states or open-hearted inquiries can enhance our spiritual journey. By welcoming their guidance into our lives, we open ourselves up to transformative experiences that expand our consciousness and set the stage for personal ascension. In your own practice, consider setting intentions that invite wisdom from beyond. A simple meditation under the vast night sky could serve as a bridge to that ethereal guidance you seek.

5. Experiences of Contact

5.1 Documenting Your Experiences

Keeping a record of your UFO experiences is not just important; it is essential for deep reflection and growth. When I first began my journey into the world of UFOs, I quickly realized how fleeting these encounters can be. A sighting might be vivid in the moment, but the details can easily slip away from memory like grains of sand. Writing down what I experienced helped me to capture the essence of those moments. It allows me to revisit the emotions, the sensations, and the revelations I felt. This reflection can provide insight and clarity, enhancing my understanding of my experiences as I grow. It also serves as a visceral reminder of those extraordinary moments that often go misunderstood by the outside world. In a field where skepticism often prevails, having documented evidence of my encounters strengthens my resolve and affirmation of the reality I have witnessed.

Throughout my experiences, I have developed various methods for documenting my journey that I have found extremely effective. One of my preferred methods is journaling right after an encounter. This involves sitting down with a pen and notebook or typing on a device, allowing my thoughts to flow freely without self-censorship. I focus on capturing every detail, from what I saw to how it made me feel. Using a dedicated notebook for my UFO experiences not only keeps these accounts organized but also creates a tangible collection of my journey that I can return to. I've also discovered the value of using audio recordings when I'm unable to write immediately. Talking through my experiences can sometimes reveal thoughts and emotions I may not articulate on paper. Additionally, incorporating visual aids like sketches or maps can help me remember specific locations or formations that were significant during an encounter. Relying on multiple forms of documentation not only enriches my reflection but also makes my experiences come to life in ways that text alone might not achieve.

As you consider how to document your own experiences, remember that there is no one right way to capture your journey. It's about finding what resonates with you and makes your experiences meaningful. Experiment with different methods, whether they be journaling, recording, or even creating visual art inspired by your encounters. The aim is to create a record that speaks to your journey, providing a resource for introspection and growth. Keeping track of your experiences not only aids in personal understanding but also connects you to a community of others who share similar paths. Developing this habit can turn the ordinary into the extraordinary and imprints your unique journey on the tapestry of ufology. Take immediate action right after an encounter—no matter how small or fleeting it seems—because those moments can catalyze profound insights as you move forward in your journey.

5.2 Interpreting Messages and Symbols

Decoding messages and symbols encountered during contact is an essential aspect of the journey towards ascension and understanding the presence of UFOs. These messages can manifest in various forms, such as flashes of light, specific colors, or even patterns that seem to repeat during sightings. For me, the first time I experienced this was during a night of stargazing when a bright flash outshone the stars for just a moment. Initially perplexed, I later learned that such flashes could represent communication attempts from otherworldly beings. It opened my mind to consider what they might want to convey and inspired me to research indigenous interpretations of celestial phenomena. The interplay of intuition and reason guided my efforts to grasp what these symbols represented. Paying attention to the feelings that surfaced alongside these encounters often revealed deeper layers of meaning.

Reflecting on personal experiences, there was a night when I was meditating under a starlit sky. Suddenly, I felt an overwhelming urge to focus on a particular constellation. Coincidentally, within minutes, I noticed a series of movements aligned perfectly with it. Every sequence appeared deliberate, as if they were dancing to some cosmic rhythm solely for me. Afterward, I spent time contemplating the connection between my feelings and those celestial events. This led me to understand that the symbolism of the constellation resonated with my life path, representing guidance and hope. Such moments illustrate the importance of journaling our experiences, for they can often reveal insights we're initially too close to see.

One practical tip I can share is to create a dedicated space for reflection and interpretation after an encounter. Bring out tools such as a journal or art supplies to express what you felt and saw, as engaging with the symbols creatively can often unlock meanings that are hidden in the conscious mind. Trust that intuition can lead to revelations that blend the rational with the spiritual, offering you a profound understanding of your experiences and the messages they carry.

5.3 The Emotional Journey of Contact

Experiencing contact with UFOs brings a whirlwind of emotions. I can still vividly recall the moment I first gazed at an unidentified craft hovering above me. My heart raced with a mix of fear and exhilaration. In one split second, curiosity surged through me, and I felt a profound connection to something far beyond myself. This rollercoaster of feelings is natural and perhaps even necessary as it immerses us in the depths of our own humanity. The highs and lows of such experiences can lead to moments of pure ecstasy followed by intense doubt and confusion.

As I navigated this emotional landscape, I learned that every feeling plays a role in my spiritual growth. Embracing the fear, the wonder, and the uncertainty allowed me to peel back layers of conditioning I didn't even know I held. Even the moments of doubt became essential, guiding me toward deeper self-reflection. I discovered that it's okay to feel a whole spectrum of emotions, from euphoria to anxiety. Accepting and embracing these feelings can lead to profound enlightenment, offering insights into not just the universe but also ourselves. This journey of emotions is not just about the contact with extraterrestrial life, but also about connecting more deeply with our own hearts and spirits. Finding peace amidst emotional chaos is a wonderful skill that can empower us on our path.

Be gentle with yourself as you experience this emotional journey. Journaling can be a powerful tool, a way to process your feelings and thoughts. Writing down your experiences can help you reflect on your emotions, understand your fears, and celebrate your breakthroughs. Remember that every feeling is a guidepost on your journey. Allow them to lead you deeper into your own spiritual awakening, and you'll find that the universe is not only outside of you but also within.

6. Astral Travel and UFO Connection

6.1 Techniques for Successful Astral Projection

Astral projection is an exhilarating journey that can help expand our consciousness and alter our perception of reality. To facilitate successful astral travel experiences, I discovered a variety of techniques that truly resonate. One technique that I found particularly effective was the practice of deep relaxation. I would find a comfortable position, often lying flat on my back, and focus on releasing tension from my body. Each breath I took deepened my relaxation, allowing me to sink into a state where the physical world began to fade away. Visualization played a crucial role, too. I would imagine a bright light above me, inviting me to surrender into its warmth, while picturing myself gently rising out of my physical body. This combination set a solid foundation for my astral adventures.

As I delved further into these techniques, I encountered my fair share of challenges along the way. My first attempts were met with frustration and doubt. I vividly remember a night where I felt stuck, unable to separate from my body. I was discouraged, questioning if I had the ability at all. But as I persevered, I learned the importance of patience and belief in the process. Through consistent practice, I gradually built confidence and resilience. Celebrating the small victories was essential. Each time I managed to enter that relaxed state, I anchored myself in the experience, knowing I was inching closer towards successful projection.

My triumphs were often marked by moments of vivid clarity and unexpected revelations. One particular experience remains etched in my memory. I felt myself lifting effortlessly, spiraling through what felt like layers of existence, overwhelmed by the beauty of it all. I encountered entities that felt ethereal yet familiar, as if they were guiding me in my journey. With every successful astral projection, I became more attuned to the vibrations surrounding me, the intuitive whispers guiding my exploration. Embracing this connection allowed me to access deeper realms of knowledge. A practical tip that helped me immensely was to keep a journal of my experiences. Writing down the details not only enhanced my understanding but also reinforced my intention, propelling my astral journeys forward, opening doors that I never knew existed.

6.2 Meeting Extraterrestrial Beings in the Astral Realm

During my astral journeys, I have encountered several fascinating extraterrestrial beings that have profoundly influenced my spiritual understanding. These experiences often begin in a serene state, as my consciousness begins to expand beyond the physical realm. On one occasion, while floating through a colorful kaleidoscope of energy, I suddenly found myself in the presence of a tall, ethereal figure. Its skin shimmered in shades of blue and silver, radiating warmth and wisdom. Without speaking, this being transmitted knowledge directly into my mind. I felt an overwhelming sense of peace and unity, as if I was part of something much larger than myself. These encounters feel sacred and leave an indelible mark on my spirit, as if I am not just a witness but an integral participant in a cosmic dialogue.

The wisdom gained from these interactions is astonishing. Each meeting offers insights that transcend earthly concerns, shedding light on the mysteries of existence and our connection to the universe. I remember one instance where I was guided to understand the concept of harmonics—how every being vibrates at a unique frequency. The extraterrestrial shared that when we align ourselves with these frequencies, we open doors to higher dimensions of consciousness and understanding. Many messages emphasize the importance of love, compassion, and the interconnectedness of all life. They often remind me that our thoughts and emotions shape our reality, encouraging me to focus on positive energies to foster a better world. These teachings resonate with ancient wisdom found in various spiritual traditions and affirm my belief that we are all part of a universal tapestry of life.

Being open to these experiences requires a willingness to expand our perception and embrace the unknown. Practical steps for those interested in connecting with these realms include setting clear intentions before sleep or meditation, creating a peaceful environment, and engaging in grounding practices afterward. Keeping a journal of your experiences can also help you recall the insights gained during these astral travels. Embrace the mystery, trust your intuition, and remember that the universe is vast, filled with knowledge waiting for you to discover.

6.3 The Intersection of Dreams and UFO Experiences

Dreams often serve as a mysterious gateway to realms beyond our physical existence, and they can provide insight into UFO phenomena in ways we might not fully comprehend. The mind, in its infinite creativity, has the ability to tap into experiences and knowledge that are often hidden from our waking consciousness. Many individuals who have encountered UFOs describe their experiences as surreal, almost dreamlike, suggesting that the realms of dreaming and UFO encounters may share more in common than we realize. Through my own experiences, I've begun to see dreams as a potential bridge to understanding these otherworldly encounters. In particular, certain dreams have fused elements of UFO sightings and extraterrestrial beings, creating a vivid tapestry of imagery that blurs the line between reality and imagination. Reflecting on these dreams offers a unique lens through which we can analyze and interpret UFO phenomena.

In one of my most vivid nocturnal experiences, I found myself aboard a spacecraft, suspended in a timeless void. The atmosphere was rich with an electric energy that felt both familiar and otherworldly. I could see ethereal beings moving gracefully through the ship, guided by a light that pulsated with a rhythm I couldn't comprehend. This dream left an imprint on my consciousness long after I awoke. It felt as though the experience was more than just a figment of imagination; it carried the weight of reality, as if a door was opening to a deeper understanding of the universe. The images were powerful, packed with symbols that seemed important yet elusive. I often ponder whether these dreams serve as a form of communication from intelligences beyond our physical realm, calling me to expand my awareness and explore the mysteries of the universe.

As I continue to explore the intersections between dreams and UFO experiences, I encourage others to keep dream journals and actively reflect on their nighttime journeys. The insights we gain may not come through the conventional means of logic and reasoning, but they can guide us toward a greater understanding of our connection to the cosmos. Embrace these nocturnal adventures, for they could very well lead to revelations that illuminate our path toward ascension and a deeper engagement with the unknown.

7. Community and Support

7.1 Finding Like-Minded Souls

Surrounding myself with supportive individuals has been one of the most vital aspects of my journey toward ascension and summoning UFOs. It's easy to feel isolated when you delve into topics that many may view as unconventional or even fringe. Having a network of like-minded souls offers encouragement, alternative perspectives, and a sense of belonging. These supportive connections can provide comfort during challenging moments and motivate you to keep exploring and growing. Each time I've connected with someone who shares my fascination, I've felt a boost in my energy and determination to pursue my path. Whether it's through casual conversations or deep discussions about our experiences, these interactions remind us that we are not alone in this journey.

Finding such communities, both online and offline, can be rewarding yet challenging. Start by exploring social media platforms like Facebook, where groups dedicated to UFO summoning and spiritual ascension thrive. Reddit is another gem, with subreddits focused on various aspects of the phenomenon. Don't hesitate to engage in these spaces; share your thoughts and ask questions. Local metaphysical shops often host events or gatherings, which can be a fantastic opportunity to meet others in your area. Even attending workshops or seminars on spirituality can introduce you to kindred spirits who understand your interests and aspirations. If you are feeling particularly adventurous, try reaching out to local organizations or clubs that focus on the unexplained. You may be surprised at what you discover.

One practical tip is to create a vision board or a list of the qualities you seek in a community. This can clarify what you want from your interactions and keep you focused as you seek those connections.

Remember, the universe responds to your intentions, and by being proactive, you'll draw in those supportive individuals who are just as eager to explore and expand their understanding of the cosmos.

7.2 Sharing Your Experiences: Online and Offline

Encouraging open dialogue about UFO experiences in safe spaces can transform individual journeys into collective understanding. There is something incredibly liberating about finding a group of people who can relate to your experiences. When you share stories about sightings or strange encounters, it often opens the door for others to share their own. Online forums and local meet-ups dedicated to these discussions create an environment where people feel safe expressing their thoughts without fear of judgment. I have found that when people talk openly, they can uncover deeper insights about their experiences and connect on a level that feels almost telepathic. These spaces not only validate personal experiences but can also foster a sense of community, making the sometimes lonely quest for understanding a shared journey.

Reflecting on my own journey, I remember the first time I shared my UFO sighting in an online forum. I was nervous, my fingers hovered above the keyboard as I crafted my post. Would people believe me? To my surprise, the responses were overwhelmingly supportive, and many shared their own stories. This exchange not only brought me comfort but also ignited my passion for exploring and understanding these phenomena further. I also made some lasting friendships through these discussions. When I faced skepticism from friends and family, it was this community that provided me with the encouragement and understanding I needed. They offered a safe haven where I could explore my curiosity and delve into discussions about ascension and the universe.

As I continued to engage with the community, I learned the importance of sharing experiences both online and offline. Regularly attending local UFO meet-ups helped reinforce my understanding of these mysteries.

Hearing firsthand accounts from like-minded individuals filled me with inspiration and courage. Each story was unique, contributing to a tapestry of knowledge and connection that felt expansive. I discovered that whether in an online forum or gathered in a physical space, sharing experiences is not just about anecdotal evidence—it's about creating a network of support that elevates our individual journeys towards discovery. If you find yourself yearning to share your story or hear others, seek out local groups or online communities that resonate with your experiences. You'll find that your voice has the power to inspire others, just as theirs can enrich your own understanding.

7.3 The Role of Community in Spiritual Growth

Community plays an integral role in the expansion of our spiritual understanding. My journey into the realms of ascension and summoning UFOs has shown me that when we gather with like-minded individuals, our collective energy amplifies our intentions and insights. Each person brings their unique experiences and knowledge to the table, creating a rich tapestry of shared wisdom. When we meditate together or engage in group practices, the vibrations seem to heighten, and it's as if we tap into a larger source of universal energy. This shared journey creates a sense of belonging and fosters an environment where exploration and growth become not only possible but also deeply rewarding.

Exploring collaborations and collective energy reveals how powerful elevated summoning experiences can be. I remember the first time I joined a gathering focused on connecting with extraterrestrial energies. We began by aligning our frequencies through deep meditation, with each participant sharing their intentions. The atmosphere was charged with excitement and openness, creating a channel for experiences that transcended the ordinary. As we focused our minds and hearts on the task, I felt a collective pulse, a synchronization that opened the door to encounters that felt almost surreal. This synergy not only deepened our personal experiences but also cultivated a profound sense of trust and connection within the group, elevating our practices to multidimensional realms that we could hardly have accessed alone.

Gathering in community settings for collective spiritual practices serves not only to enhance our individual journeys but also to shape the larger narrative of our spiritual evolution. As I reflect on these experiences, one practical tip comes to mind: seek out or form a group that resonates with your spiritual aspirations. Whether it's through local meet-ups, online forums, or workshops, the bonds formed can lead to profound encounters and insights. Remember, the energy of community truly has the power to elevate your spiritual growth and summon experiences that are beyond what you might imagine on your own.

8. Raising Your Vibrational Frequency

8.1 The Science Behind Vibrational Frequencies

Delving into the science of frequencies and their impact on our surroundings reveals a fascinating interplay between energy, matter, and consciousness. Everything in the universe is made up of energy, vibrating at specific frequencies. Even the air we breathe, the ground we walk on, and the objects we interact with emit their own unique frequencies, each one influencing the environment around us. Through a deeper understanding of how these frequencies work, we can begin to appreciate not only how they affect the physical world but also how they resonate with us on a personal level. When we tune into our own vibrational frequency, we can experience profound shifts in our emotions, health, and ultimately our reality. This connection to frequency goes beyond just the physical; it aligns with our thoughts, feelings, and intentions. Every time we express love, joy, or gratitude, we are raising our vibrational frequency, which can create ripples in our environment and affect those around us.

Connecting the dots between personal frequency and experiences with UFOs opens up a captivating perspective on those encounters that many have had. I've found that moments of heightened awareness or spiritual elevation often coincide with sightings of unidentified flying objects. When I was in a particularly meditative state, I noticed a distinct shift in my perception, almost as if my frequency had aligned with something otherworldly. This connection suggests that beings from other dimensions or advanced civilizations might interact with us at different vibrational levels. The more we elevate our consciousness, the more likely we are to perceive and connect with these unexplained phenomena. Many individuals report similar experiences, noting that their UFO sightings often occurred during times of intense emotional or spiritual growth. It's as if these crafts are sensitive to our energy, responding to our frequency and inviting us to expand our awareness of the universe.

Being mindful of our own vibrational frequency can enhance our ability to attract extraordinary experiences, including those elusive UFO encounters. Practicing meditation, engaging in breathwork, and surrounding ourselves with uplifting energies can truly elevate our vibration. Pay attention to the energy in your surroundings, the people you interact with, and the thoughts you cultivate. By intentionally forming a positive state of being, you can open doors to experiences beyond the ordinary. The universe is a vast tapestry woven with energy and frequency, and we are all interconnected threads. As we explore this connection, we empower ourselves to not only understand the science behind vibrational frequencies but to actively participate in the greater cosmic dance.

8.2 Practices for Daily Vibration Enhancement

Daily practices play a significant role in raising my vibration, and I've found several that have proven effective over the years. One of the most impactful practices has been meditation. I dedicate at least 20 minutes each morning to sit in silence, focusing on my breath and tuning into my inner self. During this time, I visualize a bright light surrounding me, filling me with positive energy. Another approach that I cherish is spending time in nature. Whether it's a walk in the park or simply sitting by a tree, immersing myself in the natural world reconnects me with the vibrant energies of the Earth, which naturally elevate my frequency. I also incorporate sound healing into my routine; listening to frequencies such as 528 Hz can profoundly shift my vibration, allowing me to align with the universe's harmonious energy.

Finding personalized routines that resonate with you is essential because each person's journey is unique. Experimenting with different practices can help you discover what truly uplifts your spirit. Consider journaling as a way to explore your thoughts and feelings, which can sometimes reveal insights that raise your vibration. You might also want to try affirmations. Speaking positive statements out loud can shift your mindset and enhance your energy. Remember to pay attention to how you feel during these practices, and trust your intuition to guide you towards what feels right. This personal evolution is a part of the process of ascension, and customizing your routine is key to connecting with the energies you wish to summon.

As you explore these ideas, consider keeping a vibration journal. Documenting your daily practices and noting how they affect your energy levels can be a powerful tool in finding what works best for you. Over time, you'll create a personalized set of routines that not only raise your vibration but also support your unique spiritual path.

8.3 A Higher Frequency Lifestyle: Diet, Exercise, and More

Exploring lifestyle choices that contribute to sustained higher frequencies has been a transformative journey for me. It's fascinating how our daily habits can impact our energy levels and spiritual ascension. I found that simple adjustments in my lifestyle created powerful shifts in my vibration. For instance, cultivating a routine that prioritizes mindfulness has helped me maintain a connection to the subtle energies around me. Practices like meditation and yoga not only calm the mind but also help raise my vibrational frequency. Living in harmony with my surroundings, being attuned to the cycles of nature, and seeking out uplifting experiences have all contributed to a more elevated state of being. Understanding the vibrational impact of my thoughts, emotions, and actions has been a crucial aspect, showing me that everything is interlinked. Surrounding myself with positive, like-minded people reinforces this higher frequency, creating a supportive environment for my spiritual practices.

Diet and exercise have played pivotal roles in supporting my spiritual practices. I realized early on that what I put into my body significantly influenced my energy levels and my ability to connect with higher consciousness. A plant-based diet rich in whole foods like fruits, vegetables, nuts, and seeds nourished not just my physical body but also my spirit. These foods resonate at a higher frequency, allowing me to feel more light and energetic. Hydration became equally important; drinking pure, clean water helped clear mental fog and supported my physical vitality. Exercise, particularly practices that encourage breath and movement such as running or dancing, allowed me to release stagnant energy and invite fresh, vibrant energy into my life. These physical practices have not only strengthened my body but have also deepened my spiritual connection, creating a perfect synergy that supports my journey towards ascension.

Maintaining this higher frequency lifestyle is not merely about adhering to a strict schedule; it's about cultivating a conscious approach to each day. Having rituals that ground me, whether it's a morning routine of gratitude and intention-setting or an evening reflection practice, keeps me aligned with my purpose. Every thought, every bite of food, every breath becomes an opportunity to enhance my vibrational state. As I continue to explore and share these experiences, one practical tip that has proven valuable is to incorporate moments of stillness throughout the day. Even a few moments to breathe deeply and center myself can elevate my energy and open the channels for connection with the higher realms, making the process of ascension more profound.

9. Nature's Role in UFO Summoning

9.1 Connecting with Nature: A Spiritual Anchor

Nature has an extraordinary ability to heal and restore, acting as a spiritual anchor in our busy lives. When I step outside, I often find myself enveloped by the gentle whispers of trees and the soothing presence of flowing water. Just being in that environment can ground my spirit, helping me to reconnect with my inner self. I recall a time when I sat quietly by a river, the sound of the water punctuating the stillness around me. It was as if the river was washing away my worries, allowing me to focus on the spiritual work I was engaging in. The fresh air and vibrant colors of the landscape often prompt a deeper meditation, facilitating a connection to the universe that feels both comforting and enlightening. Grounding myself in this way amplifies my intentions and thoughts, letting me merge with the energy of nature. I truly believe that when we integrate these natural surroundings into our spiritual practices, we are aligning ourselves with a greater force and enhancing the sanctity of our work.

During my journeys seeking UFO contact, nature played an invaluable role in these mysterious experiences. There were nights I stood alone in open fields, gazing up at the starlit sky, feeling a deep sense of belonging to the cosmos. On one particular evening, I set out beneath the vast canopy of a sprawling forest. Surrounding myself with trees and the earthy scent of pine created an atmosphere ripe for contact. The stillness of nature heightened my senses, making me acutely aware of every sound and movement. I remember watching fireflies dancing around me, their flickering lights reflecting the messages I hoped to receive from beyond. It was in these moments that I felt the connection between Earth and the universe the strongest. Often, the more I sat in quiet contemplation within nature, the more aligned I felt with the energies of other realms.

Each experience deepened my understanding of how vital it is to maintain this connection to nature if I am to successfully navigate the spiritual journey towards making contact with UFOs.

One practical approach to merge your spiritual practices with nature is to schedule regular times to immerse yourself in natural settings. Whether it's a park, forest, or beach, find a spot that resonates with you and allows for tranquility. Bring along tools for meditation, such as crystals or journals, and dedicate time to absorbing your surroundings. As you begin this process, remain open to messages and experiences that may come your way; the universe often communicates in whispers and subtle shifts in energy. By cultivating this space for reflection and connection, you may find your spiritual journey enriched with new insights and perhaps encounters that defy explanation.

9.2 Natural Locations that Enhance Summoning

Throughout my journey in exploring UFO summoning, I've encountered various natural sites that have proven to be particularly conducive to these experiences. One such place is the high desert of Sedona, Arizona. The stunning red rock formations have a unique energy that seems to pulse with life, drawing not only hikers but also those seeking connection with the cosmos. During my time there, I set out on a starry night, feeling a deep resonance with the surroundings. The stillness of the night, combined with the vastness of the night sky, created an atmosphere ripe for a summoning experience. The magnetic fields in this area are said to enhance people's energy, making it easier to connect with higher frequencies.

Another location that I found riveting is Mount Shasta in California. This majestic peak boasts a sacredness that many feel upon arrival. There's an ancient lore surrounding Mount Shasta, with many tribes and cultures regarding it as a portal to the stars. My personal encounters here were profound. I climbed to a quiet spot on the mountain, surrounded by towering trees and the soft whisper of the wind. I could feel the earth's energy swirling around me, and as I closed my eyes, I sensed a deeper connection to the universe. This connection felt like a gentle pulse, urging me to reach out and summon the celestial beings I sought.

When attempting to summon UFOs, tuning into the energy of a location can significantly enhance the experience. My encounters in places rich with natural vibrancy, like the ancient forests of the Pacific Northwest or the open plains of the Midwest, have shown me that these environments naturally amplify one's intentions. Each experience is a reminder that the world is filled with energy, waiting to be harnessed. Next time you seek to summon, consider choosing a location known for its unique energy. Trust your instincts about where to go, and prepare yourself to tap into the vastness of the universe surrounding you.

9.3 Communing with Elemental Spirits and UFOs

There is an undeniable connection between elemental spirits and UFO phenomena that invites deeper exploration. Whenever I find myself in the presence of nature, whether it's the rustling leaves of a deep forest or the gentle waves of the ocean, I can feel a certain energy. Elemental spirits, beings tied to the elements of earth, air, fire, and water, exude a vibrancy that resonates with the unseen forces of the universe. Over time, I began noticing how these spirits often appear in conjunction with strange lights in the sky and unexplained phenomena. Both elemental spirits and UFOs seem to hint at the same universal truth — that we are all interconnected within a web of energetic beings. Engaging with these elemental energies enhances my awareness and perception, drawing me closer to the mysteries of the cosmos.

To commune with these energies effectively requires intention and mindfulness. I have found that creating a sacred space is foundational in establishing a connection. This could be as simple as sitting quietly in my garden, setting an altar under the stars, or even meditating in a natural setting. Focused intention is crucial; I visualize a bridge formed between myself and the elemental spirits. This visualization helps me feel the nuances of their presence. I often invite elements by chanting or using sounds that correspond to the particular energy I wish to connect with. For instance, the soft whisper of wind through trees can be a gentle invitation to the air spirits. Another technique involves deep breathing exercises that align my energy with the natural rhythms of the universe. Once in a focused state, I try to send a clear request into the cosmos, allowing the energies of both elemental spirits and UFOs to respond to my call. It's in these moments of deep respect and attunement that I have experienced the most profound encounters.

Having spent years honing this practice, I recommend keeping a journal of your experiences. Documenting details about your interactions helps track patterns in your connections with both elemental spirits and UFOs. You might uncover recurring themes, symbols, or emotions tied to your communing sessions. Additionally, each night outdoors beneath the stars with an open heart can deepen your understanding. Being patient and open-minded to the messages and experiences that transcend the ordinary is key. The next time you're out in nature, take a moment to acknowledge both the elements around you and the mysteries of the universe above. Simply being present can allow a significant exchange to unfold, leading to enriching experiences and revelations.

10. Aligning with the Cosmic Energy

10.1 Understanding Cosmic Energy Patterns

The universe is filled with various energy frequencies, often referred to as cosmic energy. This energy weaves through all existence, influencing everything from the growth of plants to the flow of human emotions. Exploring the concept of cosmic energy has unveiled an intricate web connecting all living beings, suggesting that we are not separate entities but part of a greater tapestry. Have you ever felt an inexplicable shift in your mood or energy when in nature or during a full moon? Those moments reflect the powerful influence of cosmic energy on us. Understanding these energy patterns can deepen our awareness of ourselves and enhance our alignment with universal rhythms. Acknowledging how external cosmic forces affect our internal world can be a transformative experience, paving the way for spiritual ascension and expanded consciousness.

Through my experiences, I've come to understand that engaging with cosmic energy requires intention and openness. When I began to actively seek out moments of energy alignment—like practicing mindfulness or participating in group meditations—I felt a deeper connection to not only myself but to the collective consciousness. There's an undeniable synergy when individuals gather with the desire to tap into these energies. The more I explored, the more I realized that each of us can hone our abilities to detect and interact with cosmic energies, guiding us towards deeper revelations and spiritual insights. Consider integrating simple practices into your daily life, like visualizing light surrounding you or meditating under the stars. Each small step deepens your connection and illuminates the path to ascension and the wondrous experiences that lie ahead.

10.2 The Connection Between Astrology and UFO Summoning

Astrology offers a unique lens through which we can understand the cosmic energies at play in our lives, particularly when it comes to practices like summoning UFOs. I've often found that the alignment of celestial bodies can significantly enhance my attempts to connect with otherworldly beings. For instance, during the full moon, the heightened energy seems to intensify my meditative practices. The lunar phase amplifies intuition and psychic capabilities, making it a powerful time for setting intentions and summoning experiences that transcend our earthly existence. Similarly, aligning my summoning attempts with favorable planetary transits, such as when Mercury is in retrograde, has provided clearer communications during my sessions. Each time these astrological events occur, I can feel a palpable shift in my energy, as if the universe is aligning its forces to facilitate my connection with UFOs.

Reflecting on my own astrological chart has revealed insights that are deeply relevant to my UFO journey. My sun sign, which influences my core identity, is in a position that promotes innovation and exploration. This has encouraged me to step outside conventional beliefs and embrace the search for extraterrestrial experiences. The houses in my chart also play an essential role. For instance, having significant placements in my ninth house, the house of higher learning and spiritual exploration, indicates a natural inclination toward understanding the unknown. Through careful study of my chart, I have realized that certain transits trigger meaningful events, such as sightings or contact experiences. The day I conducted a summoning ritual lined perfectly with a solar eclipse in my birth chart, which seemed to unlock an entirely new level of interaction with the universe.

Connecting astrology to UFO summoning isn't merely about observing celestial events; it's also about understanding oneself and how cosmic energies interact with our personal journeys. I encourage readers to explore their own charts. Look for the placements of planets and signs that might indicate a fascination with the unknown. Noticing the cycles and phases of the moon or planetary movements can reveal optimal times for your own summoning practices. By aligning your intentions with these astrological influences, you may find a deeper connection to your spiritual path and an enhanced ability to summon the extraordinary.

10.3 Harnessing Energies of Solar and Lunar Phases

The solar and lunar cycles have always held a special place in spiritual practices and summoning. As I dived into these cosmic rhythms, I realized how profoundly they can influence our intents and energies. The ebb and flow of the moon can correlate with our emotional states and our connection to the universe. For instance, during the new moon, energies are ripe for beginnings and intention-setting, as the darkness allows for the planting of seeds—both in the physical and spiritual realms. Conversely, the full moon symbolizes release and culmination, offering a time to let go of what we no longer need and to celebrate the achievements we've made. These celestial events can align so powerfully with our summoning practices, creating opportunities to connect with higher vibrations and, perhaps, even entities from beyond our earthly realm. I found that the intensity of the solar energies can amplify the results of our rituals as well. The vibrant energy of a solar eclipse, for example, can act as a catalyst for transformation, magnifying our desires into the cosmos.

Timing is everything when it comes to effective summoning practices, and aligning these rituals with the solar and lunar phases can significantly enhance our experiences. I learned to observe the cycles closely, marking the new and full moons in my calendar as sacred opportunities for connection. When working with the new moon, I prepare myself with meditation and reflection, focusing on what I wish to manifest. This is the ideal time to create vision boards or write intention lists, directing my energy towards what I want to bring into my life. As the moon grows, I find it helpful to engage in rituals that involve calling in energies, which can include chanting, invoking spiritual guides, or even using crystals that resonate with the growing lunar energy. During the full moon, I shift my focus towards gratitude and release, often conducting rituals where I burn or bury papers filled with things I wish to let go of. This cathartic act feels like a cleansing, allowing me to make room for new energies to flow in.

Practicing these aligned rituals has brought deeper insights and connections. It's beneficial to educate oneself about the astrological aspects that accompany these phases. Knowing whether the new moon is in a fire, earth, air, or water sign can influence the energies at play and help refine our intentions. I've found using a lunar calendar helpful, as it illustrates not only the phases but also the corresponding zodiac signs. Each sign carries its own characteristics, guiding how we can best work with the energies presented. Engaging deeply with these cycles transforms how I approach my ascension practices. The connection to the cosmic rhythms serves as a reminder that we are part of something greater than ourselves. As we tap into these energies, we open ourselves to enhance our summoning capabilities, inviting cosmic entities into our space while fostering our growth within the universe.

11. The Role of Sound and Frequency

11.1 Sound Healing Techniques for Increased Awareness

Sound healing techniques offer transformative ways to raise consciousness and open channels to higher frequencies. These methods, deeply rooted in ancient practices, tap into the vibrational essence of sound to align our energy states. When I started exploring these techniques, I discovered how different frequencies could evoke profound shifts in my awareness. Using Tibetan singing bowls, for instance, helped me quite literally resonate with a deeper sense of self. The rich harmonics of the bowls seemed to vibrate through me, creating an inner landscape that felt more expansive and connected to the universe. These tools didn't just create soothing sounds; they sparked an awakening within me, sharpening my senses and elevating my consciousness to levels I had never imagined.

My personal journey with sound healing took an unexpected turn as I delved deeper into my experiences with UFO contact attempts. During those moments of stillness, enveloped by sound, I often found myself in a state of heightened awareness. I remember lying on my mat, surrounded by the gentle hum of crystal bowls, when I felt an undeniable pull to the outside world. It was as if the vibrations were opening a portal, connecting me to something beyond our physical existence. I sensed a presence, an energy that intensified with the subtle fluctuations of sound around me. Each note seemed to resonate with an unseen force, amplifying my intuition and inviting interaction. It's fascinating how sound creates a bridge between realms, making us attuned not only to ourselves but also to the intelligence that lies beyond our earthly experience. When you allow sound to guide you, it can be a powerful catalyst for extraordinary encounters.

For anyone looking to explore this connection, I recommend setting aside time for personal sound healing sessions. Create an environment that feels sacred and safe, using instruments like tuning forks, chimes, or even your voice. Focus on your breath as you immerse yourself in the sounds. As you do this, keep your intention clear, whether it's for healing or to deepen your connection with otherworldly beings. Allow the vibrations to wash over you and observe any sensations, messages, or insights. This practice can foster an awareness that transcends the ordinary, drawing you closer to experiences that may lie beyond your current perception.

11.2 Using Music for Summoning

Music has a profound ability to evoke emotions and shift energy, which is why it plays a crucial role in the summoning process. The rhythms, melodies, and vibrations of specific tracks can help set a powerful atmosphere conducive to connecting with higher dimensions or inviting extraterrestrial beings. My journey began when I realized that certain sounds and frequencies heightened my sensitivity to the energies around me. I found that ambient music, characterized by its ethereal sounds and flowing structures, can create an inviting space for potential encounters or ascension experiences.

There's something about the way harmonious vibrations resonate with our own energy that seems to open a channel. Often, I would play specific tracks softly in the background during my meditative practices or summoning rituals, noticing how the music guided me deeper into my state of consciousness. I felt more aware of subtle shifts happening in my environment. It is not just about the sound; it's about how the music can create an emotional landscape that invites the unknown to reveal itself. Each experience became a symphony between myself and the universe, where the music acted as a conduit, connecting me to other realms.

As I delved deeper into the practice, I began to curate playlists specifically tailored for summoning and ascension. Genres like ambient, drone, and psychedelic music became staples in my exploration. Artists such as Brian Eno, with his ambient masterpieces, or the organic textures of soundscapes created by groups like Sigur Rós, were integral to my practices. I would often find myself lost in the swirling ambiance while tuning into the energies and frequencies that felt aligned with my intentions.

For more uplifting and expansive experiences, I turned to shamanic drumming tracks, which have a heartbeat-like quality that can ground the soul while also facilitating a journey into higher realms. Fine-tuning my playlists, I discovered that even certain classical pieces, like those from Debussy or Satie, can evoke a sense of yearning or longing that is useful for opening pathways to deeper connections. My collection became a living entity, ever adaptable to my emotional state and the type of contact I sought. If you are interested in incorporating music into your summoning practices, consider starting with soundtracks and genres that resonate with you personally, allowing your intuition to guide you in selecting tracks that evoke the desired energy.

A practical tip is to create a playlist with a mix of preferred genres. This way, when you're ready to summon, the music is already curated to your tastes and needs, setting the stage for a successful experience.

11.3 The Impact of Silence in Spiritual Growth

Silence has a unique power. It creates a space for reflection and connection that often goes unnoticed in our busy lives. In the stillness, where our thoughts can settle and the external noise fades away, we find clarity. This is where insights bubble to the surface, nurturing our spiritual growth. When I embrace silence, I enter a different realm. It is in those moments of quiet that I can genuinely listen—not just to the world around me but also to the whispers of my own heart. The power of silence allows me to strip away distractions, to peel back the layers of clutter that fill my mind. It's a sanctuary where I can connect with my deeper self, tapping into a well of intuition and wisdom that much of the time lies dormant. The experience becomes almost tangible, as if the universe itself is holding its breath, waiting for me to unlock the door to my own inner sanctum.

Reflecting on my personal journey, I can pinpoint several breakthrough moments that emerged from these serene periods of contemplation. One particular instance stands out in my memory—a night spent alone under a vast, starry sky. Surrounded by silence, every sound seemed amplified. I could hear the gentle rustling of leaves, the soft whispers of the wind, and my own heartbeat becoming the rhythm of the universe. In that moment, a profound realization washed over me. I understood that my connection with the cosmos was not just a distant dream but a living, breathing reality that I could tap into when I quieted my mind. The breakthrough was exhilarating. I left that night with a heightened awareness of the energies around us, convinced that silence was not simply the absence of sound, but a gateway to profound truths.

As I explore further in my spiritual practice, I've come to see the need for silence as crucial to my growth. It allows me to gather thoughts, question beliefs, and unearth deeper mysteries that surround not just my existence, but the universe itself. A useful tip is to carve out intentional moments of silence in your day. Whether it's through meditation, taking a solitary walk in nature, or simply sitting in a quiet room, let go of the urge to fill every moment with noise. When you embrace that stillness, you'll likely discover insights that can propel your spiritual journey forward, revealing the enchanting connection we have with the cosmos.

12. Overcoming Fears and Doubts

12.1 Identifying and Confronting Your Fears

Many people have a set of fears tied to the idea of UFO encounters and spiritual practices. These fears can range from the fear of the unknown to anxiety about what might happen if we open ourselves up to higher realms of consciousness. When considering the notion of summoning, fear can often creep in. The thought of connecting with extraterrestrial beings or accessing unseen realms can trigger deep-seated fears, stemming from cultural narratives that associate the unknown with danger. It's common to feel a sense of trepidation about losing control or the potential for negative experiences. I discovered that understanding these fears is the first step toward confronting them.

My journey into summoning and exploring these higher dimensions was not without its hurdles. Initially, I was plagued by fears that seemed insurmountable. I worried about what I might attract or whether I would be capable of handling the energy exchanges. However, I learned that facing these fears head-on was essential. I began to visualize the summoning process as a conversation with beings of a higher vibration rather than a confrontation. This shift in perspective empowered me. I replaced fear with an exhilarating sense of curiosity and excitement. I sought guidance from like-minded individuals and immersed myself in practices that reinforced my intuition. Each time I faced a fear, whether through meditation or other forms of exploration, I emerged stronger and more connected. This was a pivotal moment in embracing the potential of summoning and understanding my own fears as part of the larger journey.

As you embark on your own exploration of UFOs and spiritual practices, remember that fear is a natural part of the process. A practical tip is to start by writing down your fears as they come to you. By acknowledging them, you create a space for understanding. Reflect on each fear and consider its source. Is it a personal experience or something influenced by media? Then, visualize confronting that fear, recognizing it as an opportunity for growth. This act of facing your fears can transform them, allowing you to embrace the unknown with courage and curiosity.

12.2 Building Confidence in Your Abilities

To enhance confidence in our spiritual abilities and the art of summoning UFOs, it is crucial to develop specific strategies that resonate with our individual experiences. Visualization has been particularly powerful for me. I often find a quiet space, close my eyes, and picture myself surrounded by bright energy, connecting with higher frequencies. The more I practice this, the more real it feels, and my belief in my abilities grows stronger. Another method that has supported my journey is to create a personal ritual around the summoning process. This could be as simple as lighting a candle, playing some calming music, or sitting in meditation at the same time every week. By formalizing these practices, they become sacred, and my confidence deepens each time I engage in them. I also encourage journaling during this process. Noting your experiences, thoughts, and insights not only helps track your progress but also reinforces your journey, showing just how far you've come.

Affirmations play a monumental role in building self-belief, and I've found that repeating positive statements about my abilities helps rewire my thinking. Phrases like I am capable of connecting with higher realms and I trust my intuition to guide me on my path have echoed in my mind during moments of doubt. Speaking them out loud, especially with conviction, creates a ripple effect in my consciousness. Additionally, engaging in practices like yoga or grounding exercises helps keep me centered and connected to my body, fostering a strong sense of belief in what I can achieve. I always set aside time for gratitude, reflecting on moments where I've felt connected or sensed a presence around me. This gratitude not only amplifies the positive energy but also builds a profound trust in my abilities. As I continue to explore these avenues, I realize that confidence is not just a destination; it's an ongoing journey that evolves with each experience.

As I dive deeper, embracing the unknown has proven to be an essential part of this process. Allow yourself to be open to surprises; each UFO sighting or spiritual experience is a validation of your potential. Trust in the divine timing of your journey and remember that setbacks do not diminish our capability. Instead, they can serve as stepping stones towards growth. Sharing these experiences with like-minded individuals can also provide encouragement. Whether through community gatherings, online forums, or workshops focused on ascension and summoning, surrounding yourself with positive influences can bolster your confidence. If there's one practical tip that I have found invaluable, it's to celebrate even the smallest successes along the way. Each step forward, no matter how minor, is a reason to feel proud and further fuels our journey of self-belief.

12.3 Sharing Doubts: Healing Through Conversation

Sharing fears and doubts can be one of the most healing experiences we encounter on our journey. In the realm of ascension and even in discussions about UFOs, it's common to harbor feelings of uncertainty or skepticism. These emotions often bubble beneath the surface, creating a weight that can feel too heavy to carry alone. When I finally began to express these feelings in a safe and supportive environment, I found a profound sense of relief. Engaging in open conversations with like-minded individuals allowed me to see that I wasn't alone in my fears. Instead of feeling isolated in my beliefs or experiences, I discovered a community that understood my struggles. We created a space where it was okay to voice our uncertainties without the fear of being judged. This simple act of sharing helped to lift a veil off my perspective, allowing me to breathe more freely and embrace strange phenomena with an open heart and mind.

One particular conversation stands out vividly in my memory. I was sitting in a dimly lit café with a friend who shared my fascination with the unexplained. As we sipped our drinks, the talk turned to our personal experiences with UFO sightings and our hopes for ascension. I hesitated for a moment, wondering if I should share my recent doubts about the authenticity of some events I had witnessed. But as I listened to my friend recount their own experiences — filled with hope and wonder, but also tinged with hesitation — I felt a nudge to share. The moment I voiced my concerns, something remarkable happened. My fears dissipated in the warmth of the conversation, and I could see my friend nodding in understanding. This exchange not only validated our feelings, but it also sparked deeper questions and reflections within both of us. We began to brainstorm ways to engage with our fears more constructively, perhaps by attending workshops or joining discussions with even larger communities online. Healing can happen when we realize that our conversations can open doors to greater understandings and shared growth. I've learned that deep, honest exchanges can spark insights and lead us to explore new avenues of thought. Our talks transformed my fears into powerful exploration tools, fueling my desire for knowledge and connection.

Encouragement lies in genuine vulnerability. When you allow yourself to share fears and doubts, you invite others to do the same. Seek out spaces where open dialogue is welcomed, be it local gatherings or online platforms. Engage with others who share your interests, and be brave enough to express your uncertainties. You may find that healing does not come from having all the answers but from being part of a conversation that helps guide you toward discovery.

13. Documenting Your Journey

13.1 The Importance of Keeping a Journal

Journaling plays a crucial role in tracking spiritual growth. Over the years, I've come to realize that writing down my thoughts, experiences, and reflections gives me clarity and a deeper understanding of my journey. Spiritual growth can often feel like a nebulous concept, but when I put my emotions and insights onto paper, I can see patterns emerge that might otherwise go unnoticed. Each entry serves as a snapshot of where I was at that moment—what I felt, what I struggled with, and how I perceived the universe around me. These written records have documented subtle shifts in my mindset and spirit, reminding me of my progress even during times when I felt stagnant or unsure.

Effective journaling is an art I've honed over the years, and I'd love to share some tips that have worked wonders for me. First, I find that consistency is key. Whether I write daily or weekly, having a routine helps create a safe space for my thoughts. I prefer to write at the same time each day, whether in the morning light or under the stars at night, allowing the rhythm to guide my reflections. When writing, I don't worry about grammar or structure; it's the honesty of the words that matter most. I let my thoughts flow freely, sometimes even asking open-ended questions that lead me down unexpected paths. This practice often sparks epiphanies about my spiritual quests or my encounters with otherworldly phenomena. I also incorporate sketches and symbols that resonate with me, as my spiritual context isn't limited to just words.

Maintaining a journal doesn't just track spiritual growth; it also enhances my experiences in the cosmos. Whenever I summon UFOs or delve into the mysteries of the universe, I note these occasions meticulously. Recording details like the date, location, emotions, and any signs I may have perceived makes it easier to discern connections over time. I can reflect not just on what happened, but on its significance. Each journal entry becomes a component of an evolving narrative that deepens my connection to the unfamiliar. A practical tip for anyone starting this journey is to create dedicated sections in your journal. Perhaps one for spiritual reflections, another for summoning experiences, and yet another for personal thoughts. This way, when you revisit your writings, you can easily follow the threads of your development, making everything feel more connected and purposeful.

13.2 Creative Expressions: Art and UFOs

Art serves as a powerful medium for expressing emotions, ideas, and experiences that often defy conventional understanding. When it comes to UFO phenomena, art can transform what is often seen as an elusive encounter into something tangible and relatable. Through painting, sculpture, writing, or other forms of creative expression, artists can explore the feelings that accompany such extraordinary experiences—fear, wonder, confusion, and awe. I have often found that depicting my encounters with the unknown allows me to process and understand them on a deeper level, giving voice to experiences that are sometimes met with skepticism or disbelief. Each brushstroke or written word becomes a bridge, connecting the inexplicable with human emotion, revealing how deeply intertwined our realities can be. This exploration helps not only the artist but also the viewer or reader, creating a shared space for reflection and dialogue about these mysterious phenomena. Art becomes a window into an expansive universe where these encounters can be acknowledged and validated.

My own artistic journey began as a response to my UFO experiences. Years ago, while standing beneath a starlit sky, I witnessed a craft move silently across the horizon, its lights pulsating in a vivid dance. That moment was seared into my memory, and I felt an overwhelming urge to capture it. I started with simple sketches, channeling the emotion and the awe of the encounter onto paper. Over time, my passion grew, leading me to create large canvases filled with vibrant colors and abstract shapes that reflected not just the craft but my internal landscape during those moments of connection. Each piece I have created serves not only as a record of my experiences but also as a conversation starter, inviting others to share their stories and perceptions. Through my art, I have explored themes of connection and the vastness of the cosmos, and I find that this medium allows people to engage with the idea of UFOs beyond mere speculation.

To embrace your own creative expressions linked to UFO phenomena, consider allowing your feelings to flow freely. Whether you paint, write, or create music, focus on expressing the emotions connected to your experiences. You don't have to be an expert or have formal training; the most important aspect is authenticity. Pay attention to the little details of your encounters, the emotions they evoke, and the questions they raise. This practice not only nurtures your creativity but also deepens your awareness and connection to these extraordinary experiences. Bringing your feelings into your artistic practice can open new doors to understanding and perhaps even lead to insights about your own journey in the realm of the unknown.

13.3 Sharing Your Journey: Blogs and Social Media

Sharing your journey through digital storytelling is a powerful way to connect with others who are on a similar path. When I first started exploring the world of UFOs and ascension, I never expected the impact that sharing my experiences would have on both myself and others. Writing blogs or posting on social media platforms allows you to document your thoughts, feelings, and insights in real time. This process not only helps you reflect on your own journey but also encourages readers to engage with their own experiences. The stories shared can resonate with others, leading to a sense of community and shared purpose. When you open up about your challenges, discoveries, and even the moments of doubt, you invite others to do the same. It's amazing how many people are on this quest for knowledge and understanding, and by sharing your narrative, you help to create a supportive space where everyone can feel heard and inspired.

The feedback I've received through social media has profoundly shaped my journey. It's incredible to see how community interaction can amplify your experiences. When I post a new insight or question about a phenomenon, the responses often include recommendations, personal stories, or even scientific explanations that I hadn't considered. Engaging with readers not only broadens my perspective but also strengthens the bond within our community. Through comments and shares, I've met many like-minded individuals eager to explore the unknown with me. This feedback loop fosters a sense of belonging and validation that is truly motivating. Each interaction feels like a contribution to a larger conversation about the mysteries of the universe, enhancing my understanding while encouraging others to share their unique experiences. In a way, we become co-creators of this learning journey, collaborating to shed light on the celestial phenomena that intrigue us.

For anyone interested in sharing their own narratives, consider starting small—perhaps with a blog post about a recent encounter or insight that moved you. Utilize platforms like Instagram or Facebook to share bite-sized anecdotes that invite dialogue. Always remember that your voice matters and that your story can inspire others. Share your journey authentically, and don't shy away from vulnerability, as it creates genuine connections. Seek out hashtags related to UFOs and ascension to expand your reach and discover a wealth of stories from others. Engaging in this shared experience can foster an enriching dialogue that may even guide you deeper into your own journey.

14. Lessons from the Stars

14.1 Messages from UFO Encounters

Throughout my journey, I have encountered various experiences with unidentified flying objects that have left lasting impressions on my understanding of existence. These encounters are not just fleeting moments of wonder; they often carry profound messages that resonate deeply with us. I remember one night when a glowing sphere hovered silently above my backyard. In that surreal moment, I felt an overwhelming sense of peace and unity. It was as if the universe was communicating something essential to me, a reminder that we are all connected beyond the physical realm. Many have reported similar experiences, where they feel an expanded awareness or receive insights during such encounters. These messages often urge us to reflect on our purpose in life, the importance of love, and the interconnectedness of all beings.

Encouraging receptiveness allows us to glean the lessons the universe is eager to share. It's essential to cultivate an open mind and heart, inviting in the teachings that these extraordinary experiences present. I find that when I reset my perspective, moving past skepticism and embracing curiosity, the universe responds in kind. Whether through meditation, quiet contemplation, or even spontaneous inspiration during a UFO sighting, staying open invites the necessary shifts in consciousness. Remembering these moments can ground us and offer guidance as we navigate our personal paths. Practicing mindfulness can help us stay attuned to these lessons, as the synchronicities in our lives often signal the presence of something greater at play, urging us to pay attention.

As you explore the possibility of summoning your own encounters or simply wishing to understand the messages presented in the cosmos, consider adopting rituals or practices that enhance your connection to the universe. Whether it involves star gazing, using crystals, or manifesting intentions, find what resonates with you. Trust that each experience, no matter how small, can contribute to your journey of ascension and understanding. By remaining open, you allow the whispers of the universe to guide you and enrich your life in ways you have yet to imagine.

14.2 Spiritual Lessons Learned from Contact

Reflecting on the spiritual lessons I've integrated from contact experiences reveals a profound transformation within me. Each encounter has left an indelible mark, teaching me about the nature of existence and the interconnectedness of all beings. One of the primary lessons centers around the importance of love and compassion. These experiences have shown me that love is a universal language, transcending physical boundaries and cultural divides. In moments of contact, I felt a potent energy that resonated deeply within, reminding me that we are all extensions of a greater consciousness. It prompted me to reevaluate my intentions and cultivation of love in my daily interactions, further deepening my spiritual journey.

Discussing the significance of these lessons in my overall spiritual journey, I recognize that they have been game changers. They have shaped my understanding of reality and my place within it. The encounters served as catalysts for my growth, pushing me to embrace a higher perspective. Each lesson learned has acted as a stepping stone, guiding me to seek a more authentic expression of my spirituality. Moreover, the lessons of unity and humility persistently echo through my thoughts, urging me to contribute positively to the collective consciousness. Embracing these teachings has filled me with an unwavering sense of purpose, encouraging me to share insights gained from these experiences, and creating a ripple effect that inspires others on their ascension journeys.

One practical tip to integrate these spiritual lessons into your life is to create a daily practice of reflecting on your intentions. Spend a few moments each day in quiet contemplation, asking yourself how you can express love and compassion in your interactions. This simple yet powerful exercise can transform your perspective and strengthen your connection with the universe, opening doors to new insights and deeper understandings.

14.3 Integration of Cosmic Wisdom into Daily Life

Bringing cosmic insights into our everyday living is not just an ethereal concept; it is a practical journey that we can embark on with intention. One way I have found to weave these cosmic understandings into my daily routine is by establishing a morning ritual that connects me with the universe. Each day, as the sun rises, I take a moment to appreciate the vastness of existence. I practice deep breathing while visualizing the energy of the cosmos flowing through me. This intentional act allows me to ground myself and set a mindful tone for the day ahead. Whether it's through meditation, connecting with nature, or simply embracing silence, these moments of reflection help me to align my daily actions with the cosmic perspective I strive to embody.

I often reflect on how these cosmic principles can enhance our perceptions of daily life. For instance, I incorporate the idea of synchronicity into my interactions. The more I pay attention to the signs—like seeing repeated numbers, feeling a particular resonance with certain conversations, or experiencing unexpected opportunities—the more I recognize that the universe is communicating with me. This awareness transforms mundane moments into profound experiences. I recall a particular day when I was feeling lost in my work and received an unexpected message from an old friend. It wasn't just a catch-up conversation; it felt like a universal nudge, reminding me of my purpose and the connections that enrich my life.

In my own life, integrating this cosmic wisdom often manifests in small yet impactful ways. For example, I embrace gratitude not only for the big events but also for daily occurrences. Keeping a gratitude journal has helped me track the subtle gifts from the universe, reinforcing a mindset of abundance. On particularly challenging days, I turn to affirmations that resonate with my higher self, reminding me of my potential and the vast love that surrounds me. These simple practices have become essential threads in the fabric of my existence, helping me navigate life with a sense of purpose and cosmic awareness. A practical tip for anyone looking to integrate cosmic wisdom into their daily lives is to set aside just a few moments each day for reflection or meditation and to remain open to the signs and synchronicities that guide you.

15. The Future of UFO Summoning and Spirituality

15.1 The Evolving Landscape of Contact Experiences

Current trends in UFO summoning show a fascinating shift in perception. People are no longer viewing UFOs merely as symbols of science fiction or government secrets. Instead, there's a growing interest in the spiritual and metaphysical aspects of these encounters. Many individuals are actively engaging in practices aimed at inviting extraterrestrial contact, such as meditation, visualization, and energy work. This shift not only highlights a transformation in belief but also the rise of community among those who share these experiences. Social media platforms overflow with stories of personal encounters, methods for summoning, and even collective gatherings aimed at creating an energetic field to attract these crafts. The people involved often report feelings of heightened awareness, unity, and purpose, suggesting that these interactions resonate deeply within our collective consciousness, igniting a form of ascension that transcends traditional understanding.

Looking toward the future, I believe the nature of contact experiences will continue to evolve in profound ways. As technology advances and our understanding of consciousness expands, the methods of summoning UFOs may shift towards more refined and less physical means. Imagine a world where thought and intention could instantly create a bridge to these otherworldly entities. This could lead to an age where individuals no longer depend on physical gatherings or specific rituals, but operate from a place of innate connection. I envision a landscape where each of us could tap into a collective frequency, drawing forth not just UFOs but friendly entities who wish to share their wisdom. The implications of such a shift are staggering. It might not just be about seeing lights in the sky but about fostering a dialogue with consciousnesses that challenge and inspire our own evolution.

Practical steps can be taken to attune ourselves to these possibilities. Beyond the conventional methods, incorporating daily practices such as breathwork, lucid dreaming, or grounding techniques can elevate our energetic states. Engaging in these activities fosters not only personal growth but can accelerate the collective readiness for contact. By embedding these experiences into our daily lives, we cultivate an environment ripe for cosmic communication, making us not mere observers but active participants in the unfolding narrative of our universe.

15.2 Predictions for the Next Decade

There's a palpable excitement swirling around the potential developments in UFO and spiritual movements as we venture into the next decade. I have often felt the energy shifting around us, like the world collectively holds its breath, waiting for a revelation. Reports of UFO sightings are increasingly frequent, and they seem to ignite a spark of curiosity and hope among people. The dialogues surrounding extraterrestrial life have gone from whispers to widespread discussions, permeating our culture through documentaries, podcasts, and social media. As we delve deeper into consciousness exploration, it's clear that more individuals are awakening to their spiritual abilities, and this could lead to a profound collective ascension.

As we anticipate these shifts, I encourage you to be an active participant rather than just an observer. Embrace the changes and engage with the spiritual or UFO communities. This can be done through meditation, participation in group gatherings, or even creating your own rituals and practices. Connecting with others can amplify your own energy and intentions, making the process of transformation both powerful and fulfilling. By contributing your voice and energy, you help shape the narrative and play a crucial role in driving these movements forward. The world is ripe for exploration, and now is the time to unleash your curiosity, tap into your intuition, and summon your own experiences of the extraordinary.

In preparing for the future, remember to remain open-minded and maintain a learner's attitude. Balance skepticism with wonder, as this will allow you to navigate the complexities of rising phenomena with clarity. Keep a journal of your experiences and insights—this practice can help ground your thoughts and keep track of any shifts within you. As we collectively rise, the insights you gather may not only illuminate your path but also inspire others who look to you as a beacon during these transformative times. Equip yourself with the mindset of a co-creator, as the universe is ever-expanding, and we have the power to influence our destiny.

15.3 Your Role in the Cosmic Community

Recognizing our individual contributions to the cosmic experience is crucial. Each of us carries a unique piece of the universe within us, and our actions resonate far beyond our immediate surroundings. When I first began exploring the concept of ascension and the mysteries of UFOs, I realized that I was not just a passive observer but an active participant in this grand cosmic narrative. Every thought, emotion, and intention I project into the universe contributes to the collective consciousness. This interconnectedness is something we must embrace. Whether it's through meditation, communication with otherworldly entities, or simply spreading positive energy, our collective experience blossoms when we each bring forth our unique light.

Stepping into our roles as ambassadors for positive change is necessary for this cosmic community to thrive. I have taken it upon myself to embody this role actively, encouraging others to do the same. It starts with our daily interactions, infusing kindness and compassion into our lives. We can participate in group meditations to raise the collective vibration or hold space for others to explore their connections with the cosmos. The more we express our dreams and aspirations, the more we uplift those around us. Inviting others to join this journey fosters a sense of belonging, and together we ignite a powerful wave of transformative energy that resonates throughout the universe.

When each of us acknowledges the part we play in this vast cosmic tapestry, we contribute to the fabric of reality in meaningful ways. A simple act of kindness or an open-hearted conversation can ripple through the cosmic waves, influencing what we might not even see. Engaging in this shared mission encourages us to manifest our highest potentials. I often remind myself that the universe listens, and by projecting love and positivity, we can create connections that lead us to higher states of being. Today, consider starting small—take a moment to visualize the positive change you want to see in your life and in the universe. Let that vision guide your actions.

Also by Jessie Contreras

Messages from the Stars: A Guide to Summoning the Galactic Federation

Celestial Awakening: Ascension and the Art of Summoning UFOs

Energy Vortexes: Harnessing Power for UFO Summoning

The Alien Code: Unlocking the Matrix

The Ultimate UFO Summoning Guide:2026 Edition

How To Master The Ancient Art Of Summoning Motherships

The Resonant Universe: Bioelectrical Energy And The Call Of UFOs

UFOs and the Art of Mimicry: The Hidden Intelligence Behind the Disguise

About the Author

Jessie Contreras is a dedicated researcher of unidentified aerial phenomena whose work blends disciplined observation with an interest in how human consciousness shapes extraordinary experiences. Guided by a lifelong fascination with the night sky, he shares his insights through community work, educational content, and continued study. His mission is to explore the phenomenon with clarity, integrity, and an unwavering commitment to understanding what lies beyond the familiar.

About the Publisher

Summon UFOs is a forward-thinking publishing brand dedicated to exploring the intersection of consciousness, extraterrestrial contact, and human potential. Through its works, the brand presents innovative perspectives on UFO phenomena, blending experiential practices, emerging technologies, and esoteric knowledge into a cohesive framework for understanding and initiating contact. Summon UFOs aims to inspire curiosity, expand awareness, and empower individuals to engage with the unknown in a structured, intentional, and transformative way.